KYRGYZ KALPAK

RISBEK
RICHARD HEWITT

ILLUSTRATIONS BY
Nurbek Nogorbekov

Сонун Жер
Sonoon Jer

УДК 821.51
ББК 84 КИ7-4
    Х 98

      Рисбек Ричард ХЬюитт
Х98   Kyrgyz Kalpak. -Б.:2008. -

      ISBN 978-9967-25-272-1

This book was first published under the title КАЛПАК.

Risbek

КАЛПАК

ISBN 9967-422-30-1 (Russian)
ISBN 9967-429-33-x (Kyrgyz)

Х 4702300100-08
ISBN 978-9967-25-272-1

УДК 821.51
ББК 84 КИ7-4
© Ричард ХЬюитт,
2008.

Contents

DEDICATION

This book is dedicated to Amantur (Standwell) who stood well after the crash. May your people also stand well through every trial they face. I also dedicate this book to all who wear the white kalpak.

Forward

I am a descendant of the wild Anglos and treacherous Saxons who are some of the wildest, cruelest, and darkest people in world history. We are responsible for killing, raping, and enslaving many peoples, including the American Indians – a people very similar to the honorable and noble Kyrgyz. My people are worse than the Russians, who are also responsible for the historical massacres of many of your fathers. I cannot cover my shame. A deep sense of regret, sorrow, and shame grips my heart. I ask you, my Kyrgyz hosts, to forgive me, and my fathers, and my brothers for the sins we have committed against you, and your fathers, and your brothers.

I am unworthy to write this book, and would not assume such a presumptuous task if it were not for the voice of God which called me away from the darkness of my people to the mountain of God. On the mountain I met the sacred *Kydyr* who placed a white covering over my head and over my shame. I, like most Kyrgyz, am tired of religous conflict, but I had a deep hunger to know my Maker. That day on the mountain, the sense of God's presence was so overwhelming that I knelt there and devoted my life to my Maker. Ever since that day, nature, and specifically the mountain, has been my mosque (*mechit*).

Shortly after I arrived in Kyrgyzstan, my honorable Kyrgyz host killed a lamb for me, invited me to a feast, gave me the name Risbek, and put a white kalpak on my head. I believe heaven's Lord inspired my human host. This book has also been written by my human hand, but I believe it has been inspired by heaven's king. I humbly place this simple book before you.

THE KALPAK

The kalpak is the holiest national clothing for Kyrgyz. It has mysteries that many can feel when they wear the kalpak. This ancient hat seems to connect the man wearing it with the history of his fathers and the destiny of his people. But where do these feelings come from? What is the secret of the kalpak's blessing, and where is the source of its power?

(Common knowledge about the kalpak: Kyrgyz can't kill a man with a kalpak on. Kalpaks can't be put on the ground. "If you lose your kalpak you lose your head; don't trade your kalpak or you'll trade your mind. Wear a kalpak and you won't get sick, it is warm in winter, cool in summer," Kyrgyz say. Kalpaks are laid next to your head at night, never by your feet.)

THE HEAD

The kalpak is worn on the head of Kyrgyz men, who are the head of Kyrgyz families. They are also providers and protectors. The kalpak is a symbol of the head's authority and protection over the whole family. What power does the kalpak have that causes even the greatest of Kyrgyz men through every generation to come under its authority?

THE ALA TOO MOUNTAIN

The kalpak is also symbolic of the great Ala-Too Mountains, fatherland of the sacred Kyrgyz people and considered holy by those who live in them. Visitors are enchanted by these majestic mountains and the people living in yurts on the mountain's slope far from civilization. The peaks of these great mountains remain white all year long, and water the farms, cities, and deserts of many nations in distant places.

These mountains are so holy that Kyrgyz legend says a man who has made the haj (pilgrimage) to Arabia will ask, "Is there someone who has climbed the great mountain? Is there anyone who has heard the holy bird's voice?" (*uluu toogo chikgan barby? Ular ynyn ukgan barby?*) His search seems to indicate that he is still looking for someone holier than himself – someone who has made a greater pilgrimage than the one he has just made to Arabia. Why would someone who just went to the holy desert be looking for someone who has climbed the great mountain? Is the mystery of the Kyrgyz kalpak about to reveal a secret as ancient, holy, and life giving as these great mountains?

Freedom to Think

In Chingis Aitmatov's book, "A Day Lasts Longer Than A Thousand Years," the *mankurt's* skullcap shrank and dried around the captive's head, constricting his ability to think, and ultimately making him an obedient slave to his captor's commands. Chingis Aitmatov's brilliant analogy reminds us how easily we believe destructive, foreign teachings. The *mankurt's* constricting cap is symbolic of incorrect faith in an isolated vision, narrow philosophy, or human tradition. Fear, force, manipulation, or indoctrination are used to constrict the mind's ability to think.

The kalpak is probably the best contrast of the *mankurt's* skullcap. The kalpak, which stands higher than other head coverings, is symbolic of a higher "heavenly" knowledge and broad-minded faith that incorporates the visions of many prophets, *oluyas* (saints), discoverers, scientists, and thousands of years of human history.

The space under the kalpak depicts freedom – there is no pressure (fear) applied to the head. The owner of the kalpak is free to consider different points of view. This broad-minded perspective gives him a better ability to choose his path. Such people are not guided by the dictates of the church, the *mechit*, Moscow, foreigners, money, etc., but by righteousness, kindness, wisdom, justice, and the Spirit of God.

With this freedom, we are able to experience and view the world in new ways. This higher vision will give us the ability to make new discoveries that will bless the nations. My pagan Anglo-Saxon fathers had a "kalpak" experience hundreds of years ago when they found the ancient book of Jacob's people and Manas' tribe. As my forefathers opened their minds to the faith of Jacob's Lord, the stupidest brutes on earth were transformed into the greatest inventors of the world. Their darkened minds were freed, and their inventions have blessed the world with telephones, radio, electric light bulbs etc.

Surely God gave the kalpak to the Kyrgyz, who love freedom and wisdom. But now, it seems that foreign teachers are challenging the authority of the kalpak and your freedom to think. Our world-view or religion is always the first place to be assaulted. Do you have freedom to seek God, or are you being pressed to consider only one concept of God? Figuratively, you may be wearing a *mankurt's* hat that darkens your thinking and keeps you from succeeding or from blessing other nations[1].

THE 7 RESPONSIBILITIES OF EVERY MUSLIM

In Kyrgyzstan, we can find an example of how someone has kept our minds narrow and darkened. I have read that Muslims have 7 responsibilities[2]: to believe in one God, the angels, the holy books, all the prophets, Judgment Day, destiny, and the living creation.

But these responsibilities seem to be ignored by most Muslims I've met. For example, I only know a few wise, free Muslims who honor the holy books. These Muslims have nurtured their people, kept them in their religion and broadened their minds. But many other Muslim leaders in Kyrgyzstan seem to have constricting, manmade excuses that prevent the common people from reading all God's verses and thus from obeying Him, and fulfilling their Muslim responsibility. These narrow-minded teachings have caused many spiritually deep Kyrgyz to look for God in other religions. Is it possible for the Kyrgyz to honor the Lord by offering a "white kalpak" religion that upholds all 7 Muslim responsibilities, or must we be the *"mankurts"* of

---

1 Our Faith makes us who we are; it shapes us. The Taliban in Afghanistan are formed by their faith; their faith, not necessarily their religion, makes them who they are today. It is the same with the Swiss and the Mongolians, etc.

2 Some Muslims reduce this list to 6 or 5 responsibilities, but all openly acknowledge the Muslim command for all Muslims to believe in One God, in angels, in all the prophets, and read all the holy books and believe in Judgment Day. These are the major themes of the Koran.

foreign imams who don't want us to read and understand the holy books of God? I think God is calling you to be Muslims who think more broadly and higher than other Muslims in other nations; and I think the kalpak our Creator has given you is an indication of His calling for the Kyrgyz to be great thinkers, inventors, and theologians.

THE RELIGION OF FATHER ADAM

The first and oldest of the Muslim holy books is the *Toorat* (Torah). It describes the ancient history of humanity's first fathers and is helpful for helping us discern the difference between God's true religion for all peoples and man's false, constricting, religions[3].

The *Toorat* talks about Father Adam and Mother Eve sinning against God. After their sin, they wanted to cover their shame, and so, they sewed leaves together and covered their shame with leaves. But God didn't accept this manmade, perishable, plant clothing (covering). Instead the Lord covered our parents in clothing of animal skins.

Where do you think God got the animal skin? Did God kill an innocent animal to cover the shame of our first father and mother?[4]

Breaking God's command has terrible consequences, which cannot be covered by our own work or "plant material." Humanity has a terrible history of constantly developing new religious practices that are supposed to cover our shame and make us feel and look better. But our ways are not God's ways. He doesn't accept our manmade religions. We need God's solution; we need His religion. God did the work and covered our father and mother's shame through the spilling of blood – with the sacrifice of an innocent animal's soul. The kalpak, which is made of

---

3 Koran 6:84-91, 154-157
4 Genesis 3 & Koran 7:19-32

animal material, reminds us of that first soul, which was slain to cover humanity's sin and shame. Perhaps the kalpak is a symbol of God's true religion; the first religion God gave to Father Adam.

God's Religion or Man's Religion

Now Adam knew Eve his wife, and she conceived and bore Cain and said, "I have acquired a man from the Lord." Then she bore again, this time his brother Abel. Now Abel was a keeper of sheep, but Cain was a tiller of the ground. And in the process of time it came to pass that Cain brought an offering of the fruit of the ground to the Lord. Abel also brought of the firstborn of his flock and of their fat. And the Lord respected Abel and his offering, but He did not respect Cain and his offering. And Cain was very angry, and his countenance fell. So the Lord said to Cain, "Why are you angry? And why has your countenance fallen? If you do well, will you not be accepted? And if you do not do well, sin lies at the door. And its desire is for you, but you should rule over it." Now Cain talked with Abel his brother, and it came to pass, when they were in the field, that Cain rose up against Abel his brother and killed him. (story from *Toorat* – 1Musa[5] 4)[6]

Abel seems to understand God's religion. He worships God appropriately by sacrificing an innocent animal. But Cain arrogantly offers his own *"namaz"* (worship) - a plant offering. Like the leaves that Father Adam used to cover his shame, so also Cain's plant offering is not acceptable to God. Cain obviously doesn't understand the seriousness of sin or the holiness of God, so he thinks he can come to God without a sacrifice. He only offers plant material - an offering without blood and without a soul (*jan*). So

---

5 1Musa is Genesis. This passage is from Genesis chapter 4.

6 Since many imams get very upset when the Koran is translated, I have not included Koranic verses in the text, but left the reference in the footnote.

many of the religious hats and turbans of different religions are made out of plant material. Is our Creator using this symbolism to indicate that religion still hasn't pleased God? If so, what does the Spirit of God want to indicate through the kalpak?

GOD GIVES HUMANITY A NEW START – THE FIRST NOORUZ

The heavenly books go on to describe the downward fall of man. The descendants of Father Adam eventually became so bad and dark and worthless that God decided to destroy humanity with a great flood. Humanity's sins always have terrible consequences, which bring destruction and loss of life. Only the prophet Noah and his family were saved in a great boat (ark). When the flood receded the ark rested on top of a great mountain. Noah and his family came out of the ark and offered God a sacrifice of clean animals. Humanity was given a new start on that mountaintop. It was a new era for mankind.

Is the kalpak's mountainous shape given to remind us of God's amazing mercy? He is the One who gives humanity a "new beginning" (*Nooruz*) – another chance. He is so good, because we all need a "new start". Happy *Nooruz*!

Man is Deceived Until He Meets the Kydyr

The *Toorat* says that mankind came off that high mountain to the plains. On the lowlands humanity's thoughts and faith once again became narrow and constricted. They started building a sacred tower that is really just a manmade imitation of the Lord's eternal mountain. The tower was built to exalt the name and fame of mankind. Often times man's religion is used only to exalt man. We do our religious prayers and deeds to be seen by men, not God. God doesn't accept this type of religion (*Toorat* 1Musa 11, *Injil*-Matt 6, Koran 2). These false religions, like cotton or synthetic hats, look good to other people, but have no ability to cover our shame from God's eyes or Judgment Day's terror. We need the covering that the holy books say God gives.[7]

After Noah, all the nations became pagan again. Then about 2000 years after Father Adam, God called the prophet Abraham and told him that his seed would be a blessing to the whole world. The *Toorat* says that Abraham was old and his wife was still childless when the "messenger of the Lord" came to Abraham's camp. Abraham recognized his Lord and greeted him very well, in the same way that the Kyrgyz are expected to greet the "*Kydyr Aleih Salaam*[8]". The *Kydyr* blessed Abraham and promised to give him a son through his old, childless wife (1Musa 18, Koran 11:71, 37:112). If the *Kydyr* came to you would you recognize him like Abraham did?

---

7 Koran 7:25(24), Toorat Genesis 3:21, Injil Romans 13:14

8 The "Kydyr Aleih Salaam" is a Turkic name for the eternal wandering prophet who visits everyone once in their life.

ABRAHAM & THE 2ᴺᴰ MOUNTAIN SACRIFICE

The *Kydyr's* promise to Abraham was fulfilled, and the prophet Isaac was born. Later God asked Abraham to sacrifice his promised son on a mountain. Abraham set his face toward the mountain to obey God and sacrifice his own son. He tied up his son and prepared to kill him. Then God stopped Abraham and provided Abraham with a ram. Abraham offered that ram as a sacrifice in place of his son.

Was God being cruel by testing Abraham, or was he showing humanity the real cost of our sins? Some fathers think it would be easier to die than to see their own son die. If that is the case, then perhaps God was showing us on that mountain that even sacrificing our own self would not be enough to pay for our sins or cover our shame. God is merciful and accepted token animal sacrifices, but true justice would require the spilling of blood much more valuable than the blood of animals and *Kurman Ait* lambs.

Whose blood and soul is precious enough to pay for all of humanity's sins?

Wealthy Jacob

The prophet Jacob also met with the *Kydyr* and received a great promise that his seed (descendant) would bless the whole world. Today, some people who read the holy books are amazed at the similarities between the Jacob of the Bible (*Toorat, Zabur, and Injil*) and the Jakyb of the Manas *Epos* (epic). It is very possible that the prophet Jacob and the Kyrgyz Jakyb are the same man.

There are too many similarities to mention in this small book. But the *Toorat* and the Manas *Epos* say that both Jacobs have a son named Manas[9]. Both Jacobs were wealthy, nomadic shepherds who had two wives and great herds. They were oppressed in foreign lands where they were crafty enough to increase their herds. Eventually both wealthy Jacobs came back to their fatherland. Both also prayed to the Lord of heaven and received a great promise about their offspring. And both Jacob's were deceptive at certain times in their lives. The Bible also says the tribe of Manas was taken captive to Assyria in 720 B.C. and has been missing since that time.

There are many other similarities and interesting facts that you will find between these two rich Jacobs when you read all the Muslim holy books and the Manas *Epos*.

Do you think these holy books may contain the ancient source of the Kyrgyz people's wonderful epic, spiritual culture, and the mysterious kalpak? When you put on your kalpak and fulfill your Muslim responsibility you'll find out.

---

9 In Russian it is Manassiya; in English it is Manasseh; in Turkish languages it would be Manas. The Bible says Jacob adopted Manas and Ephraim from their father Joseph. You Kyrgyz still practice this same custom to this day.

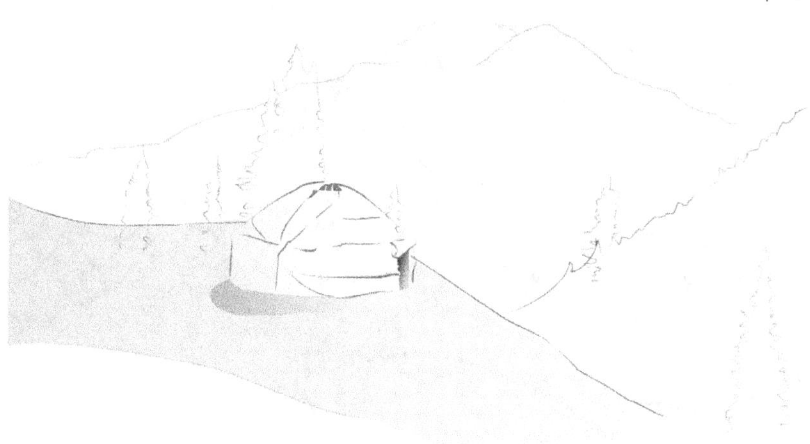

THE HOUSE OF JACOB'S GOD

One of God's prophets said, "Now it will come about that in the last days the mountain of the house of the LORD will be established as the chief of the mountains, and will be raised above the hills; and all the nations will stream to it. And many peoples will come and say, 'Come, let us go up to the mountain of the LORD, to the house of the God of Jacob; that He may teach us concerning His ways, and that we may walk in His paths." (Isaiah 2:2,3)

I like to think that the black stripes on the kalpak represent the roads which the nations will use when they come from the four corners of the earth to the mountain of the Lord and to the house (yurt[10]) of Jacob's God.

______

10 Those who read the holy books will see that the yurt is probably the mysterious "House of Jacob's God" and "Tent of David" which God will use to enlighten many nations. I hope someone writes a separate book about all the symbols in the yurt.

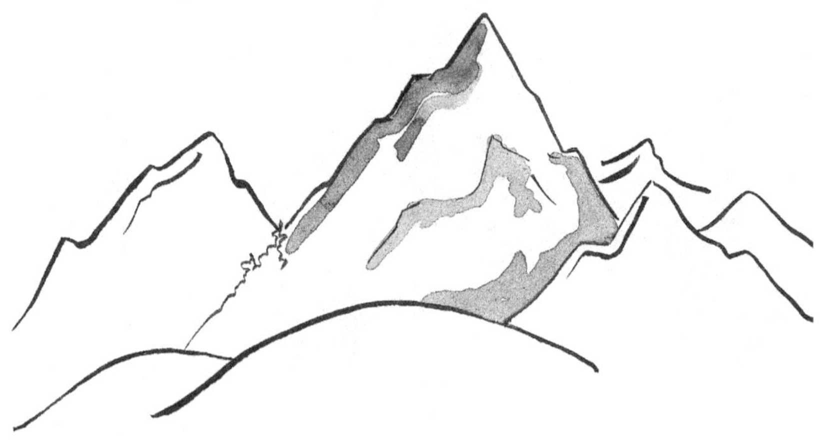

God's Third Great Mountaintop Sacrifice

All the great religions of the world have ways that they think will help them get to God. The Jews have 10 commandments, the Tengirchilik religion[11] has 7 commands, the Muslims have 5 commands, and the Christians have 2 commands. But these commands don't get us to God. On the contrary, they help us realize how far we are from God. Have you ever met a Jew who never coveted? Have you met a Muslim who always prayed 5 times a day, everyday, for all his life? Have you ever met a Christian who always loved God with all his heart, mind, and strength; and who also loved his neighbor as himself? I have never met someone who is blameless in his religion.

I have learned from the commands of all the religions that I, with all of humanity, am actually very far from God. Only when I have this humble position can I begin to see I

---

11 In this book I refer to the Tengirchilik religion as the pre-Islamic belief of the Kyrgyz. It is obvious the ancient Kyrgyz were not Muslim, but I do believe they were a circumcised people and had faith in the One True Creator God. I don't think ancient Kyrgyz were true shamanists.

need heavenly help. I need the great blessing of the *Kydyr* and the sacrifice of a lamb far more innocent and valuable than myself. Any attempt of my own to be righteous or recompense my sins would be an unacceptable "plant offering" or "perishable covering". I need a holy offering and a "kalpak" type of covering.

The commands of God have enlightened and humbled my arrogant heart. So, like Abraham, "the friend of God," I

have set my face toward the mountain of God and found that God has provided another sacrifice on the mountain that will protect people of every religion.[12] And He has invited all of humanity to feast with Him at His төлөө (payment feast) on that holy mountain.

---

12 Koran 2:63, 64

God's Table (Dostorkon)[13]

After a sacrifice there is always a feast. One of God's prophets said, "… the Lord of hosts will prepare a lavish banquet for all peoples on this mountain; a banquet of aged wine, choice pieces with marrow, and refined aged wine. And on this mountain He will swallow up the covering, which is over all peoples, even the veil, which is stretched over all nations. He will swallow up death for all time, and the Lord God will wipe tears away from all faces, and He will remove the reproach of His people from all the earth; for the LORD has spoken." (Isaiah 25:6-8)

Let's go to the Lord's mountain and feast with God, so He may take off the dark veil that is covering our nations and bring us into the brightness of his hope.

Friendly Mountain

God meets with many of the prophets on the mountain and gives them great revelations. Mountains seem to be a place where men meet God and learn how to become God's friend. The *Injil* and Koran both say that Abraham was God's friend. Some people think that God has many servants but few friends. Do you know anyone today who is God's friend?

The kalpak reminds me of the mountains where God met with his prophets and developed a deeper relationship with them – mountains seem to be the place where we fellowship with God at His table.

Don't you think God values relationship more than man's endless work and countless religious obligations? Try to develop a relationship with God and see if you can hear what He is saying to you.

---

13 Koran 5

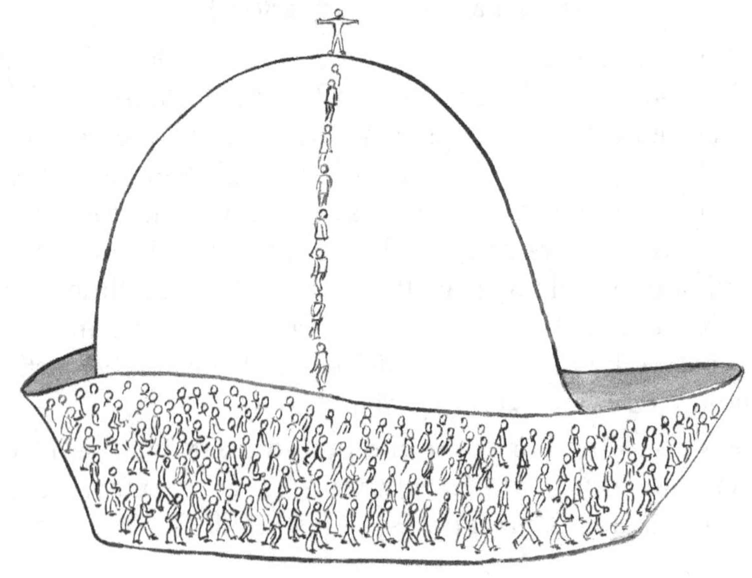

Two Roads

Remember, there are basically only two religions - only two ways: your own way or God's way; the lower way or the mountain way; the perishable way or the eternal way; the cheap, lifeless way or the expensive, life-giving way; the way of faith or the way of unbelief – you are either following man or God!

Every person is born on the lower road. We grow up in a dark world based on fear, lies and half-truths. Most people never leave this cursed, circular road. But we will all come to the intersection and look at the road that climbs the Lord's Mountain. (This is usually the time in your life when you'll meet the *Kydyr*.) Some will turn their back on the passing lusts and pleasures of our lower world and set their face toward the eternal mountain of God. Like Abraham, they seek a higher nation, whose king is God.

The prophet Jesus mentions these two different roads: *Enter by the narrow gate, for wide is the gate and broad is the way that leads to destruction, and there are many who go in by it. Because narrow is the gate and difficult is the way which leads to life, and there are few who find it* (Matt 7:13,14).

The kalpak's lower band looks like a wide road that goes around and around. This unrighteous circling is man's own, meaningless *"namaz"*. The wise Kyrgyz fathers warned us about this road. We are told not to walk around in circles.

"Oh my son, don't circle the yurt! You'll bring a curse," yells the whitebeard.

The thin stripe going up the kalpak looks like the narrow road that goes to eternal life and the feast on God's mountain. Will you be among the few who believe in God enough to leave the lower road and arrive to the heights of human existence?

THE GREAT "KURMAN AIT" FEAST FULFILLED

I have mentioned God's first great sacrifice in about 4000 B.C. and the sacrifice of Abraham in about 2000 B.C. and the ancient prophecies of the 3rd great sacrifice on the Lord's mountain. The holy books give a historical account of that third great sacrifice on a mountain about 2000 years after Abraham. This third great sacrifice is considered the fulfillment of all the other sacrifices. It is "the sacrifice on the mountain of the Lord" where mankind floats above God's judgment, is really given a new start, and our new era begins. It is on a mountain where the most priceless blood of all is sacrificed, so that humanity is perfectly justified and forgiven and our shame is finally perfectly covered. It is the mountain where we can become God's friends and celebrate with Him at the feast He has prepared for all nations, tribes, peoples, and religions.

Listen, you who are free from the *mankurt's* skullcap, listen to the most famous story on planet earth: God's perfect gift to humanity, the *Kydyr Aleih Salaam,* set his face toward the mountain and offered himself as a sacrifice. The hands that blessed so many and gave so much were pierced and eternally scarred on the pagan's shameful cross. That hole in the *Kydyr's* hand and the cross he was nailed to have forever become the symbols of the final great sacrifice and God's amazing mercy.[14] God's great love for humanity and the humble *Kydyr's* perfect submission to God are always remembered by the hole in his hand and the sign of his sacrifice on your kalpak.[15] Yes, that holy symbol is forever marked on the top of free Muslims' highest hat, the white kalpak.

Those who trust in God's eternally true religion are not condemned, because they have received God's gift – the *Kydyr*. Like Noah's family and Abraham's son, they will be protected from God's judgment and be blessed with eternal happiness and unending life. But those who reject such a great gift of grace and kindness will lose their happiness forever in the fire that is never quenched.   Like Noah's neighbors they will have no protection and nothing to cover their shame; all their own works will perish.

Just as a Kyrgyz will never harm or kill a man wearing a kalpak, so God will not damn a man who has the sign of the *Kydyr's* sacrifice over his head and soul. Thank God!

---

14 Koran 19:21

15 The sign of Jesus' cross on top of the kalpak has been mentioned by many Kyrgyz authors as being a very significant part of the kalpak's design.

THE KORAN TESTIFIES

Now we understand why the Koran powerfully reminds us that Jesus is the sign of judgment day. Can you imagine standing before God with Satan or angels accusing you of everything you ever did wrong? You can hear the screams of people being dragged into hell. You recognize the voice of one of your relatives who rejected the kalpak's heavenly revelation. He was the one who always listened to man's teaching, not God's. You weep for him and those you love. Then a book is opened that has everything you ever did wrong written in it. Devils are ready to drag you into the fire too.[16] Satan is reminding God of your worst sin and the negative effects it had on people you never met. Hell is waiting for you. Hell is hungry. You can feel its pull. God, the Judge, looks and sees that the sign of the kalpak marks you; you are one who has recognized and welcomed

---

16 Koran 40:70-72

the *Kydyr*. Your shame has been covered; your sins have been removed. You are clean and blessed before our holy Creator. God smiles at you and says, "Well done. You have overcome the world. Enter into my joy." The most amazing joy springs up from your heart as you fall down before God weeping and singing gratefulness to God that flows from a spring of joy and gratitude in your deepest soul.[17]

The *Kydyr* has robbed hell of another victim and is giving God another friend.

JESUS, THE KYDYR

God accepted the perfect sacrifice of the *Kydyr* and raised him from the grave to be seated with God in heaven. The Koran and the *Injil* (New Testament) both affirm this truth.[18]

In John's Revelation of heaven there are many times that we see Jesus in heaven as the fulfillment of the *Kydyr's* perfect number "7". Jesus also appears bright and shining as the *Kydyr* dressed in white clothes. There are many other aspects of Jesus that clearly reveal him as the *Kydyr*.[19]

Even though he is in heaven, he has appeared to many people since he rose from the dead. And one of the signs

---

17 Because of the public death threat in January 2001, I have often had to make sure I'm ready to be killed. I have fully put my trust in the *Kydyr's* eternal blessings and am sure that the righteousness and payment of his "kalpak" is over my soul. The *Kydyr* has commanded me to bless those who hate me, and *"throw food at those who throw stones"*. He is my only hope, my defense, and the one whom I desire and obey. He is my guide to heaven. It is his symbol that I wear forever.

18 Koran 3:55

19 Note: Those who compare the similarities between the Jacob of the holy books with the Jacob of the Manas Epos, will also benefit from comparing the *Kydyr* of the Manas epos and Kyrgyz folklore with the *Kydyr* of the holy books. So far I have found too many similarities to write in this small book. Could I ask some of the scientists of Kyrgyzstan to do more research on this topic? One other topic that the Kyrgyz would benefit from is an honest study comparing the ancient curses that Jacob (Israel) experienced when they sold their father's religion with the present day curses that the Kyrgyz are suffering for selling their religion and ignoring the Toorat, Zabur, Injil of their fathers.

of the *Kydyr* is his eternal wound in his hand caused by the nails that pierced him. The *Injil* depicts Jesus telling one of his unbelieving disciples to come, put his finger in Jesus' hand and believe (John 20). The hole in Jesus' hand is the symbol that helps humanity recognize him as the Messiah,[20] God's Servant, the one who perfectly submitted to God's will. He is the most perfect Muslim, the guide of Manas, the hero of Christianity, and the fulfillment of the Jewish prophets. He is the peak of every religion.

---

20 Old Catholic paintings often depict Jesus with a hole in his hand.

Road Partner

In another story from the *Injil*, some travelers don't recognize *Kydyr* Jesus when they first meet him on the road. Only after they welcomed him into their home did the travelers see, but then Jesus disappeared, as the Manas *Epos* says the *Kydyr* so often does (Luke 24). The *Injil* and Koran show many of the blessings Jesus gives as he travels from village to village. The eternal destiny of those villages is determined by how they greet the *Kydyr* (Matt. 11:20-30).

Have you ever wondered why Jerusalem has experienced so much war? Read the story of the *Kydyr* coming to Jerusalem on donkey in Luke 19:28-44. Did the Jeruslaem welcome him? Do you think Afghanistan, Tadjikstan, and Chechniya welcome *Kydyr* Jesus at this time? Could their wars be connected to their rejection of Jesus, the blessed *Kydyr*? Are they ruining the honor of all Muslims by ignoring the prophet of peace? Is present day Kyrgyzstan starting to experience the same kind of narrow-minded religion that Jerusalem had 2000 years ago and that Afghanistan has had for the last 35 years? Today seems to be the "time of visitation" for the Ala-Too Mountain? How will you respond to the prophet of peace (salaam)?[21]

You are the honorable Kyrgyz, descendants of the greatest people who ever lived; I beg you to be the best, reach for the highest, fly with wings of eagles, regain the honor of your ancient fathers and make peace between the warring peoples of this world; then you'll be the most noble Muslims of our modern times.

"May your road be blessed; may your road partner be the Kydyr."

---

21 Read the Koran and Injil and see what God does to those who don't believe Jesus.

Kydyr of the Mountain

Before *Kydyr* Jesus was sacrificed he did many things on mountains. He would pray on a mountain like Manas (Matthew 14), and He fed bread to the multitudes that followed him on the mountain (John 6). Jesus also climbed a mountain and gave advice, which reveals God's highest standards and God's ultimate intention for humanity (Matt. 5-7). Unfortunately, we are like Father Adam's and Noah's and Abraham's descendants; we turn away from the "feast" on the mountain to feed on the garbage of humanity. We reject the *Kydyr's* advice and turn to the lower darkness of manmade philosophies and religions. These lower sects can't seem to understand the significance of the mountain and the holy sacrifice. They have even blasphemed God's servant and done many things to keep people from reading the holy books and greeting the *Kydyr*. Their darkness is signified by the dark base around the lower part of the kalpak, which is contrasted against the white "mountain" part of the kalpak.

THE KYDYR DRESSED IN WHITE ON THE MOUNTAIN

Kydyr Jesus once again went up a mountain and revealed his true nature:

Now after six days Jesus took Peter, James, and John, and led them up on a high mountain apart by themselves; and He was transfigured before them. His clothes became shining, exceedingly white, like snow, such as no launderer on earth can whiten them. And Elijah appeared to them with Moses, and they were talking with Jesus.

Then Peter answered and said to Jesus, "Rabbi, it is good for us to be here; and let us make three tabernacles; one for You, one for Moses, and one for Elijah:- because he did not know what to say, for they were greatly afraid.

And a cloud came and overshadowed them; and a voice came out of the cloud, saying, "This is My beloved Son. Hear Him!" Suddenly, when they had looked around, they saw no one anymore, but only Jesus with themselves. (Mark 9:2-8)

Those who turn to the mountain of the Lord (Tengir Too) will see who Jesus really is and hear God's voice. But those who remain in the lower religions of humanity's crowded areas will never hear God above the many voices and constant noise of the world's cities and various calls to prayer and chiming church bells. Will you search for the *Kydyr* with all your heart and listen to him?

HONOR YOUR HEAD

Kyrgyz respect their kalpak. They place it high above the ground in a place of honor. Even when they sleep they will never put it on the ground or by their feet. This is symbolic of the way we are supposed to treat the head of humanity. Unfortunately, the Jerusalem's religious leaders did not honor the *Kydyr*. They betrayed him into the hands of pagans and stirred up the common people against him. Soon the whole crowd was yelling, "Crucify him! Crucify him!" Today some of society's leaders have done similar things; they are like Adam's evil son who worshipped God the wrong way. These leaders have despised the head of humanity, rejected him as pagan, and stirred up the common people against him. You also may have feared these loud religious leaders and rejected the *Kydyr* as foreign or insignificant. I understand how you feel; people have threatened me too. But don't be afraid,[22] don't be deceived, don't reject the great prophet of your fathers, and don't dishonor your head. Dishonoring *Kydyr* Jesus is a great sin, which has caused much suffering, confusion, and darkness in Kyrgyzstan.

THE PEAK OF EVERY RELIGION

Our Creator seems to be indicating by the 4 lines (roads) that go to the top of the kalpak that the pinnacle of our four great monotheistic religions come together at the peak on the Lord's Mountain.[23] The *"Ege"* of Moses and David, the *"Kok Tengiri"* of Manas and Jacob, the "Allah" of Mohammed and Ali, the "Heavenly Father" of Paul and Peter finally seem to be united in the *Kydyr* on the Lord's Mountain.

Every people and every great religion has knowledge of the *Kydyr*. In the Jewish religion he is called the *Mashayach* or referred to as "David". In the Tengirchilik religion Kyrgyz call him the *Mashayak*.[24] In Christianity he is called *Messiah* or *Christos*. In Islam he is called *Mesix*. Not only do these 4 great monotheistic religions acknowledge the greatness of the *Mashayak*, but the 4 religious books of the

---

22 Luke 12:4-7

23 Koran 5:48. Remember the ultimate standard of goodness is revealed in Jesus' speech on the mountain. Injil, Matt 5-7.

24 I have noticed that elder Kyrgyz men often think of the "Mashayak" as a conqueror or the most powerful and wise of all rulers. This concept fits the prophecies about Messiah Jesus' return at the end of the ages. The Kyrgyz concept of the *Kydyr* seems to be a gentle healer who does good and shows kindness to all. This concept is more consistent with the life-story and miracles of *Kydyr* Jesus found in the Injil and Koran. The holy books show us that the Mashayak and the *Kydyr* are one man who leads Allah's servants with mercy and destroys His enemies with fury on the last day.

Muslims also reveal his heavenly supremacy. He is the Toorat's "Descendant of Jacob through whom the nations would be blessed,"[25] the Zabur's promised "Eternal Priest and King,"[26] the Injil's promised "Living Water,"[27] and the Koran's promised "Mercy."[28] He is the Messiah. The *Kydyr's* greatness is confirmed by the kalpak that displays the 4 roads going to the *Kydyr's* place on top of the Lord's Mountain.

---

25 Gen. 28
26 Zabur 2
27 John 7
28 Koran 19:21

The Spring

Kyrgyz legend tells us that the *Kydyr* drank from the spring of eternal life and now lives forever. He blesses people in every generation and has promised this life to all who come to him and believe in him, as the verse of God says, "From his innermost being shall flow rivers of living water." The tassel on the top of the kalpak, which spurts from the center of *Kydyr* Jesus' sign like a pure spring, validates this heavenly promise and eternal truth.[29] When the nations come from the four corners of the earth to the feast on the Lord's mountain make sure they drink from the spring of eternal life. Many will come from parched lands where this water is not offered.[30] They will need your help.

Religious Divisions

In the "lowlands" of religion we hear many commands that exalt human effort and take honor from the *Kydyr*. We reduce our opinion of him to an insignificant level (i.e. an icon or foreign prophet), so we don't feel the need to listen to him. Every lie imaginable has been produced about the *Kydyr* and his word in the lower levels of every religion. These lies cause darkness that start religious wars, arguments, and terrible divisions in the "lowlands" of human thought. Far from the peak it is easy to condemn other tribes or religions for their "strange" customs and *"aram"* (unclean) behavior that is contrary to our *"namaz"* (way). This judgmental attitude is signified by the increasing distance between the lines (roads) at the lower level of the kalpak far from the *Kydyr* and a truly global perspective.[31] The further we get

---

29 The symbolism of a spring is equated with the Holy Spirit (Is. 44:3), which the Koran and Injil say is given to us as a guide to truth. I suggest that you start reading the verses of God by asking your Maker to guide you with His Holy Spirit. Also read Koran 23:50. Jesus is on a height with springs and flocks. He is the good shepherd, the living water, and the height of every religion.

30 Matt. 10:42

31 Koran 2:35,36

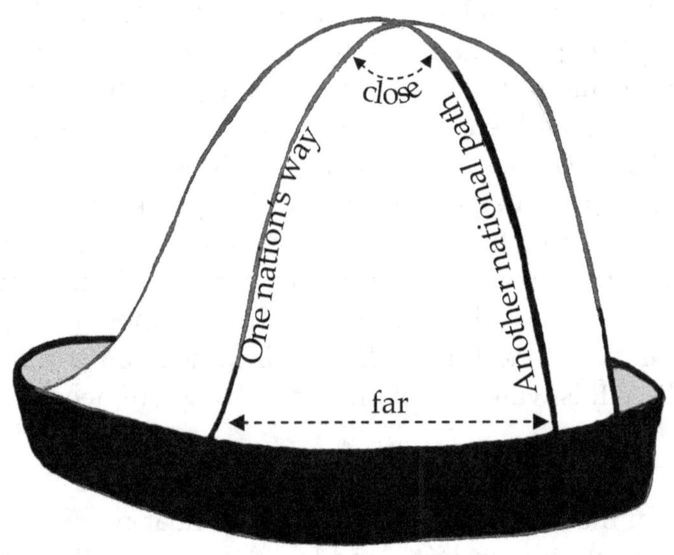

from Jesus's example, the further we get from each other and the more our world deteriorates.

But everything changes on the Lord's Mountain in the house of Jacob's God where every nation is welcomed. We become so overwhelmed by His grace and mercy for us, that we are unable to judge others. The love and forgiveness we have received from God on the mountain helps us forgive and care about others.[32] Our perspective changes from the top, and we can see much further. Only when we come to the peak of religion, the *Mashayak* (*Mesix*) of prophets a.k.a the eternal saint, can we see and appreciate the good aspects of other religions, cultures, and peoples. Only in the one

---

32 Remember the Toorat says Manas' name means "to forget" or "forgive". Isn't it amazing that the ultimate blessing of "Manas" takes place here on the Mountain of God … when we forget our grievances against each other and welcome one another without prejudices?

prophet of all religions do all the roads unite[33] and wars end. "They shall not hurt nor destroy in all My holy mountain, for the earth shall be full of the knowledge of the Lord as the waters cover the sea."[34] Would you Kyrgyz please come to the Lord's Mountain and fulfill your peacemaking role on earth.

THE ONE COMMAND, THE TRUE AZAN

While our religious teachers seem to be adding more rules and laws to our religions, and while we unsuccessfully try to do all our religious moves and washings and creeds in the lowlands, there remains a voice on the mountain that is still waiting to be heard. All religions and all their different laws, commands, and creeds are reduced to one simple word of advice for all who come to the mountain. This is God's call, this is his *azan:*

And a cloud came and overshadowed them; and a voice came out of the cloud, saying, "This is My beloved Son. Hear Him!" Suddenly, when they had looked around, they saw no one anymore, but only Jesus. (Mark 9:7,8) [35]

Notice that God does not ask you to change your religion. He simply asks you to come to the peak of your religion and listen to the one on the mountain – the prophet of peace.

Are you listening to the highest voice of all, or are you listening to the many lower voices around you?

---

33   Koran 21:91, 92 & Injil, Ephesians 2

34   Isaiah 65:25

35   The Arab concept of "son" has a very narrow meaning and implies a sexual relationship took place. So Arabs feel uneasy when Jesus is called "the son of God". This is usually not an issue for Kyrgyz who have a broader definition of the words "son" and "father". The Koran makes it very clear that the virgin conceived Jesus through the breath of God, not through a sexual relationship.

BLESSING TO THE NATIONS

Remember, my pagan fathers were given the book of Jacob, they read it, and believed in Jacob's God. The book says God promised a blessing to Jacob, "All the nations will be blessed through your seed." Somehow, a part of that blessing was given to my pagan people when they believed in the God of your fathers. Despite the pagan practices that remain among my people, they were able to provide refuge, protection, and new economic opportunities to the hurting people and war torn refugees of every nation. But that blessing wasn't originally promised to my pagan fathers, it was given to the descendants of Jacob including the tribe of Manas.

Destiny

You say you are a Muslim nation, and you seem to be descendants of the Hebrew Jacob. You have kept the secrets and stories of the Jewish prophets in your kalpak and the Manas *Epos*. There are hundreds of ancient, Christian artifacts scattered throughout your mountains and rumors that Jesus' disciple Matthew lived on Lake Issyk Kol's shore. One of your mountain regions is called "The Lord's Mountain"; you have a yurt that is very symbolic of "the house of Jacob's God" and "a house for all peoples"; and you have a holy hat that is very symbolic of God's true religion and the heights for which man was created. You have freedom to read the holy books, and develop scientific knowledge, which hypocritical religious leaders in other lands prevent. Your president has welcomed the nations here,[36] and you can prepare a feast and welcome people better than any nation on earth. The Toorat say that the name Manas means to forgive; and you have forgiven the descendants of your Soviet and Kokand oppressors better than any other nation could. Why has God shown you all this 2000 years after the great sacrifice? Could God be calling you to unite the warring nations of earth on the Ala-Too? Is the "Lord's Mountain" the place where Jew, Christian, and Muslim will finally come together? Wouldn't this fulfill the

---

36 When Kyrgyzstan accepts refugees from war torn countires you will have many people here who know nothing but war. You will need to teach these people peace and truth. I suggest you give them a kalpak when they come, and then teach them to excel in holiness. For instance, if Afghans come, show them the hundreds of verses in the Koran that command Muslims to read the Toorat, Zabur, and Injil and to believe in Jesus and all the prophets. Show them the verses in the Koran that teach about the curse the nations will receive if they don't believe all the books of God. They will then understand why their nations failed and stop blaming others for their problems. Then teach the historical and scientific truths about all the holy books. When you teach them about the *Kydyr* and the Injil they will know that we must "Give food to those who throw rocks." («таш менен урганга аш менен ур»). They will learn to forgive, be humble and walk in God's ways; and they will become real Muslims. Then the peace of the Lord's mountain will spread from Central Asia.

destiny of the Ala-Too and the promise about Jacob's seed (heir)? Don't hide your "wealth" from those in need; walk out your destiny and bless our hurting world.[37] You are called to be greater than the Switzerland of Central Asia, a refuge for the poor and oppressed; a place where the nations can learn God's ways, make peace, and be restored to health. Please, my Kyrgyz, listen to the voice on the mountain, and be whom He made you to be.

THE END

---

37 Injil, Matthew 5:5,9